THE
BEE GEES

COMPLETE RECORDINGS ILLUSTRATED

ANDREW MÔN HUGHES
&ANDREW SPARKE

Essential Discographies No.137

APS PUBLICATIONS

APS Publications
www.andrewsparke.com

First published worldwide by APS Publications in 2022

Cover photograph courtesy of NBC Television
Frontispiece photograph courtesy of ATCO Records

All images contained within the discography are from the combined collections of Andrew Môn Hughes, Lee Meadows, Frank Stiller and Reinhard Wenesch.

THE BEE GEES

The Bee Gees' story begins when Hugh and Barbara Gibb and their baby daughter Lesley moved to the Isle of Man in 1946 – Hugh was a drummer and bandleader and worked at the Douglas Bay, Metropole, Alexandra Hotels during the tourist season.

Their second child, Barry Alan Crompton Gibb, was born on 1 September 1946, while twins Robin Hugh and Maurice Ernest followed on 22 December 1949 – all were born at the Jane Crookall Maternity Home in Douglas.

Although the brothers would later recall their formative years on the Isle of Man with fondness, it proved to be a difficult period for the family. Hugh's band's work was seasonal, dependent on the summer holiday season, but during the winter, tourists were scarce, and there was far less demand. As a result, Hugh turned his hand to various jobs to provide for his family, but after nine years of hardship, the family returned to Manchester in 1955 to seek better opportunities.

The brothers took their first musical steps singing in harmony in the family home in Keppel Road in the Chorlton-Cum-Hardy district. They enlisted a couple of friends to join them and formed a group called The Rattlesnakes.

They had ambitions to perform on the stage of the local Gaumont cinema, miming to a record, as other children had been doing previously during the intervals between movies. However, as they were running to the cinema, they dropped the fragile record, and it broke – they had no option but to sing for real.

They continued making performances in the local area even when their friends lost interest, and they changed their group's name to Wee Johnny Hayes & The Blue Cats.

In August 1958, the Gibb family, now numbering six with the addition of baby brother Andy (born in March 1958), emigrated to Australia and settled in Redcliffe, Queensland, just northeast of Brisbane. The young brothers began performing at the local speedway track, where their talent was spotted by promoter and driver Bill Goode, who introduced them to Brisbane radio-presenter jockey Bill Gates.

The pair were so impressed with the young brothers' talent that they signed them to a management contract and got them some local gigs. The group needed a proper name, and it was suggested that due to the abundance of the initials B and G, the group be called The BGs.

Gates recorded them at his radio station and gave the tapes some airplay which proved popular, but as the brothers were so young, record companies were not interested in signing them to a recording contract.

They began performing regularly in Queensland's Gold Coast during the next few years, including a residency at the Beachcomber in Surfers Paradise. Through his songwriting, Barry sparked the interest of Australian star Col Joye. He helped the brothers get a recording deal in 1963 with Festival Records subsidiary Leedon Records under the name The Bee Gees.

The Bee Gees first single, 'The Battle Of The Blue And The Grey'/'The Three Kisses Of Love', was released in March 1963. Even at this early stage, the brothers' vocal talents were in demand, and they made uncredited guest appearances on many records by others during their time in Australia. Barry also had a parallel career as a songwriter, with many of his songs being recorded by local artists including Col Joye, Lonnie Lee, Jimmy Little, Bryan Davies and many others.

The Bee Gees continued to release a few singles per year, all of which flopped, but a minor hit with 'Wine And Women' led to the group's first LP, *The Bee Gees Sing and Play 14 Barry Gibb Songs*. However, by 1966 Festival Records was on the verge of dropping them because of their lack of commercial success.

At this time, the brothers met the American-born songwriter, producer and entrepreneur Nat Kipner, who had just been appointed A&R manager of a new independent label, Spin Records.

Through Kipner, the Bee Gees met engineer-producer Ossie Byrne, who produced (or co-produced with Kipner) many of the earlier Spin recordings, most of which were cut at his own small, self-built St. Clair Studio in the Sydney suburb of Hurstville. Byrne gave the Gibb brothers virtually unlimited access to his studio for several months in mid-1966. The group later acknowledged that this enabled them to improve their skills as recording artists. They recorded a large batch of original material during this productive time, including the song that became their first major hit, 'Spicks and Specks'.

However, frustrated by their lack of success, the Gibbs had been making plans to return to England for some time, and they began their return journey on 4 January 1967. While at, the Gibbs learned that Go-Set, Australia's most popular music newspaper, had declared 'Spicks and Specks' the 'Best Single of the Year'.

Before they departed from Australia to England, Hugh Gibb sent demos to Brian Epstein of NEMS, who managed the Beatles. Epstein passed the demo tapes to Robert Stigwood, who had recently joined NEMS. After an audition with Stigwood in February 1967, the Bee Gees signed a five-year contract whereby Polydor Records would release their records in the UK. Atco Records would do so in the US. Work quickly began on the group's first international album, and Stigwood launched a promotional campaign to coincide with its release.

Stigwood proclaimed The Bee Gees as 'The most significant new musical talent of 1967', thus initiating the comparison of the Bee Gees to The Beatles. Before recording the first album, the group expanded to include drummer Colin Petersen and guitarist Vince Melouney. Their first international release, 'New York Mining Disaster 1941', was an immediate hit and rose into the top 20 in the UK and US.

The follow-up, 'To Love Somebody', also made it into the US Top 20 but puzzlingly stalled at number 41 in the UK. Originally written for Otis Redding, 'To Love Somebody' has become a pop standard covered by hundreds of artists.

Bee Gees 1ˢᵗ was their first international album release. It performed well on both sides of the Atlantic, peaking at number 8 in the UK and 7 in the US.

The next single was 'Massachusetts', which became The Bee Gees first number 1 hit in 1967. It was followed by 'World' which peaked at number 7. Both songs appeared on the *Horizontal* album, released in early 1968.

Two more non-album singles followed in early 1968: the ballad 'Words' and the fast-paced guitar-driven 'Jumbo' backed with 'The Singer Sang His Song'.

Other Bee Gees chart singles followed: 'I've Gotta Get a Message to You', their second UK number 1, and 'I Started a Joke' which became their highest-charting single in the US up to that point. Both tracks were taken from the band's third album, *Idea*.After the tour and TV special to promote the album, Vince Melouney left the group due to tensions within the group and a desire to play more blues styled music than the Gibbs were writing.

Their next album was the most ambitious work yet by The Bee Gees. *Odessa* was a double album, lavishly clad in a red flock gatefold sleeve. Although only containing one hit single, 'First Of May', it is hailed by many critics as their best work.

Believing the B-side to the single, 'Lamplight', should have been the A-side, Robin felt Stigwood favoured Barry as the frontman. Disgruntled, he left the group in early 1969 tobegin a solo career.

Now down to three members, Barry, Maurice and Colin were quick to come up with a new single, 'Tomorrow Tomorrow'. It was written initially with Joe Cocker in mind, its style was somewhat different from what the record-buying public expected of The Bee Gees, and it was only a moderate success.

Meanwhile, Robin was busy working on solo material which would result in a solo album, *Robin's Reign*. His first solo single was 'Saved By The Bell', which soared to number 2 in the UK chart. It was closely followed by The Bee Gees next single, the country flavoured 'Don't Forget To Remember', which reached the same position.

Late 1969 saw the release of the first of many greatest hits packages. Best of Bee Gees reached the top 10 in the UK and the US.

While Robin pursued his solo career, Barry, Maurice and Petersen continued as The Bee Gees recording their next album, *Cucumber Castle*. They also filmed a TV special with Frankie Howerd and cameos from several other contemporary pop and rock stars to accompany the album. Petersen played the drums on the tracks recorded for the album but was fired from the group after filming began. As a result, his parts were edited out of the film's final cut.

In December 1969, Barry announced that he was quitting the group, and it appeared that the Bee Gees were finished.

Despite the break-up of the group and all three brothers moving on to pursue separate works by the end of 1969, *Cucumber Castle* was finally released in April 1970.

The solo albums Barry and Maurice decided to make instead of continuing as The Bee Gees were never released, but each did produce a single, Barry with 'I'll Kiss Your Memory' and Maurice with 'Railroad'. Barry concentrated on songwriting during the break, while Maurice starred in the short-lived West End musical *Sing a Rude Song*, alongside Barbara Windsor.

Recognising their limitations in pursuing careers as individual artists, the three brothers reunited in mid-1970. However, their reunion album *2 Years On*, which included the US number 3 hit 'Lonely Days', was an inconsistent affair that found the trio struggling to find their way artistically.

Trafalgar was the follow-up album. Released in 1971, it included their first US chart-topper, 'How Can You Mend A Broken Heart', and gave The Bee Gees their first Grammy Award nomination. Later that year, the group's songs were included in the soundtrack for the film Melody.

The group's next single was the non-album track 'My World', released in January 1972. It performed reasonably well in the UK chart and was followed later in the year by their first UK top ten hit in three years with 'Run To Me', taken from the album *To Whom It May Concern*.

The Bee Gees recorded the country-rock-styled *Life In A Tin Can* in Los Angeles but despite a strong lead single, 'Saw A New Morning', both the album and single sold poorly.

So, seemingly out of touch with what the record-buying public was currently listening to, their next album – *A Kick In The Head Is Worth Eight In The Pants* – was rejected by their record company when the lead-single 'Wouldn't I Be Someone' flopped. Only the August 1973 release of their second compilation *Best Of Bee Gees Vol. 2*, brought some timely chart success.

Stigwood arranged for the group to record their next album with legendary soul/R&B producer Arif Mardin. The next album – *Mr. Natural* – included more rock-oriented tracks, fewer ballads and a strong R&B undercurrent. The album earned positive reviews but made little impact on most of the world's charts. However, on the back of another very successful tour of Australia and New Zealand, they achieved top ten status in those countries.

In early 1975, The Bee Gees returned to the United States to Miami, Florida, with Arif Mardin in tow to record at Criteria Studios. The sessions are notable for the experimentation by Barry with a falsetto voice. Over the following three albums, this would dominate The Bee Gees' sound.

The resulting *Main Course* album was an immediate critical and commercial success and scored The Bee Gees their first US number 1 single in four years: 'Jive Talkin''. 'Nights On Broadway' followed as a top ten hit, and 'Fanny (Be Tender With My Love)' reached the top twenty.

The follow-up album, *Children Of The World,* initially proved challenging. ArifMardin was unavailable to produce, and early sessions in Los Angeles with Richard Perry were disastrous. Nevertheless, the group returned to Miami and pushed ahead with studio engineer Karl Richardson, who had worked on the *Main Course* album, at the mixing desk. In addition, Richardson introduced his long-time friend, the multi-talented Albhy Galuten, to assist him. With Barry emerging as the group's creative force, the newly forged Gibb-Galuten-Richardson production team would become one of the most successful in recording history.

The first single from the album, 'You Should Be Dancing', was another international hit and topped the chart in the US. Two more singles from the album, 'Love So Right' and 'Boogie Child', emphasised their return are more than a mere flash in the pan.

As 1977 began, The Bee Gees' chart success was bolstered by *Here At Last ... Bee Gees ... Live*, recorded during their successful 1976 North American tour in support of the *Children Of The World* album.

Whilst recording their next album, Robert Stigood asked The Bee Gees if he could use some of the songs in a movie that he was making. The film was *Saturday Night Fever*.

Fuelled by the movie's success, the soundtrack became the biggest-selling album in recording history to that point. Today, with more than 40 million copies sold, *Saturday Night Fever* is among music's top five best-selling soundtrack albums.

The album spawned three Bee Gees singles—'How Deep Is Your Love', 'Stayin' Alive', and 'Night Fever', all of which were substantial global hits, but significantly, they became three consecutive US number 1s.

Later in the year, The Bee Gees co-starred with Peter Frampton in another Robert Stigwood film, *Sgt. Pepper's Lonely Hearts Club Band*. The movie was heavily hyped before its release and was expected to be a big box office hit. Instead, however, it was savaged by film critics and flopped. The accompanying soundtrack album was likewise a disaster. However, some tracks were released as singles, including 'Oh! Darling' by Robin Gibb, which made the top 20 in the US.

Spirits Having Flown was released in February 1979. Selling more than 15,000,000 copies in the US alone, it became the group's most successful studio album ever. It generated three more American number 1 hits – 'Too Much Heaven', 'Tragedy' and 'Love You Inside Out' – this gave The Bee Gees a run of six consecutive US chart-topping singles.

To capitalise on The Bee Gees Fever, which was sweeping the nation, they embarked on an extensive concert tour of the US and Canada, with sold-out concerts in 38 cities.

By the end of 1979, disco was rapidly declining in popularity. The backlash against disco put The Bee Gees' career in a tailspin when American radio stations around the US began promoting 'Bee Gee-Free Weekends'.

Sensing that some respite was required, the brothers began writing and producing for other artists. Robin worked with Jimmy Ruffin on his *Sunrise* album, which contained the hit singles, 'Hold On To My Love' and 'Night Of Love'.

Barry meantime wrote and produced Barbra Streisand's *Guilty* album. The album reached Number 1 in both the US and the UK, as did the single 'Woman in Love', becoming Streisand's most successful single and album to date.

In 1981, the Bee Gees released *Living Eyes*, their last full-length album for RSO. Still being branded as a disco group by many American radio stations, valuable airplay was denied. The first single, 'He's A Liar', only managed to scrape into the US top 30, and the album failed to make the UK or US Top 40.

Further writing and production work in 1982 for Dionne Warwick resulted in a very successful comeback for her with the *Heartbreaker* album, which peaked at Number 3 in the UK. In addition, the title track single topped the US Adult Contemporary chart.

Kenny Rogers was the next to benefit from an album penned by the Gibbs. His 1983 album *Eyes That See In The Dark* included his duet with Dolly Parton, 'Islands In The Stream', which became the biggest-selling single in the history of the RCA label. Written by all three brothers, it reached number 1 in the US, Canada and Australia, and peaked at 7 in the UK.

Later in the year, The Bee Gees contributed five songs for the *Saturday Night Fever movie* sequel *Staying Alive*, which spawned the US top 30 hit single 'The Woman In You'.

May 1983 saw the release of Robin's second solo album, *How Old Are You?* – his first since 1970's effort *Robin's Reign*. One of the extracted singles, 'Juliet', became a huge hit in Germany where it topped the chart.

His follow-up album, *Secret Agent*, in 1984, wasn't as successful, but the single 'Boys Do Fall in Love' reached the top 40 in the US and Germany.

Barry's first solo album, *Now Voyager*, complete with an accompanying feature-length video album, fell short of commercial expectations but still yielded a US top 40 single – the Caribbean-flavoured 'Shine Shine'.

Maurice also released a solo single; the country flavoured, 'Hold Her In Your Hand' extracted from the movie soundtrack to *A Breed Apart*, which Maurice scored.

In 1985, Diana Ross recorded her album *Eaten Alive*, with songs written by the Gibb brothers and production by Barry. 'Chain Reaction' became a massive hit in the UK, Europe and Australia. Meantime, Maurice produced *Runaway*: the fourth studio album by the popular Swedish singer Carola (Häggkvist), which was very successful in Scandinavia.

Robin's fourth solo album, *Walls Have Eyes,* was released in November 1985. Despite being a commercial disappointment, all three brothers wrote and sang together on the single 'Toys'. This session led to discussions about recording the first Bee Gees studio album in six years.

In an astonishing comeback, the release of 'You Win Again' saw The Bee Gees not only return to the charts but top them in the UK, Germany, Ireland, Austria, Norway and Switzerland, and hitting the top ten in many other countries. The album from which it was extracted, *E.S.P.*, was released in late 1987 and reunited them with their long-time mentor Arif Mardin as the result of a new three-album recording deal with Warner Bros.

The Bee Gees returned to the studio in early 1988 to record their next album. Sessions had barely begun when younger brother Andy Gibb died suddenly on 10 March, five days after his thirtieth birthday, due to myocarditis – an inflammation of the heart muscle, which occurred due to a recent viral infection.

Later that year, several songs from Barry's cancelled *Moonlight Madness* solo album from 1986 surfaced on the soundtrack album for *Hawks* – a comedy film written by Barry and his friend David English.

The Bee Gees' next studio album, *One*, was released in the summer of 1989. While the album was less successful in the UK and Europe than its predecessor, the title track became The Bee Gees' first US top ten single in a decade. After the album's release, the Gibbs embarked on their first world tour in ten years: covering Europe, North America, Australia and Japan.

The new decade's first Bee Gees release was *Tales from the Brothers Gibb: A History in Song 1967-1990* – a comprehensive career-spanning box set of hits, solo tracks, B-sides, and a selection of live performances from 1989's 'One For All' tour. *In addition, the Very Best Of The Bee Gees* was released simultaneously for more casual fans.

In 1991, The Bee Gees released *High Civilization*. Despite some high-profile promotion, the album struggled in the US, but spurred on by the success of the lead single, 'Secret Love', it fared well in Europe. A successful European tour followed, with the three Berlin concerts being filmed for release on video.

The September 1993 release of *Size Isn't Everything* saw The Bee Gees' return to Polydor Records. The album was particularly successful in the UK, producing three top 30 singles – the first Bee Gees album to achieve this feat since 1979's *Spirits Having Flown*.

After a four-year break from the public eye, The Bee Gees returned yet again in March 1997. *Still Waters* became their most successful album in almost 20 years, selling over five million copies globally. Notably, the album peaked at number 11 in the US, and the first single, 'Alone', reached the top 30; it finally appeared they were again being accepted by American radio and the record-buying public.

Numerous awards across the globe accompanied the album's release. The Bee Gees were inducted into the Rock and Roll Hall of Fame in May 1997. The same year, they were also the recipients of the Brit Award for Outstanding Contribution to Music, The American Music Awards' International Artist Award of Excellence, and The World Music Legend Award for Outstanding Contribution to the Music Industry. The German Bambi Awards and the Australian Record Industry Awards also saw fit to honour them with Lifetime Achievement Awards.

Beginning a very successful series of one-off concerts branded *One Night Only* in cities worldwide, The Bee Gees performed at the MGM Grand Hotel in Las Vegas on 14 November 1997. The show was filmed for cable television and was released on both DVD/video and CD. *One Night Only* sold over six million copies worldwide and topped not only the album charts in some countries but also the DVD/video charts.

The *One Night Only* world tour in 1998-1999 played to capacity stadiums in the UK, Ireland, Australia, New Zealand, Argentina and South Africa. Their concert in Sydney on 27 March 1999 in front of 60,000 fans officially opened the newly built Olympic Stadium.

The Bee Gees closed the decade, and for that matter, the century, with another concert, but this time branded *BG2K*, at the National Car Rental Center) in Sunrise, Florida, on 31 December 1999.

The April 2001 release *This Is Where I Came In* became The Bee Gees' final album of new material as a group. The title track was released as the only single from the album, but it failed to make any real chart headway despite some positive reviews.

The album's promotion schedule included a performance at the Hammerstein Ballroom at The Manhattan Center in New York on 27 April 2001, for the taping of *Live by Request*: a television special shown on the US' A&E Network, which was released on DVD later in the year.

What would be their final public performance together occurred on 17 June 2001, as headliners of the Wango Tango festival at Dodger Stadium in Los Angeles.

On the 2002 Queen's New Year's Honours List, Barry Robin and Maurice were made Commanders of the Order of the British Empire (CBE). However, when Barry and Robin were officially presented with their awards in 2004 at a ceremony at Buckingham Palace, sadly, the third member of the trio was not there.

Maurice Gibb died unexpectedly, aged just 53, on 12 January 2003 at Mount Sinai Medical Centre in Miami Beach, Florida, from complications after surgery for a strangulated intestine. Understandably in shock, Barry and Robin initially announced they intended to carry on the Bee Gees name in his memory but later recanted this, saying they wished to retire it, leaving it to represent the three brothers together.

By unfortunate coincidence, Robin's fifth solo album, *Magnet*, was released the week Maurice died. Naturally, Robin was not in any mood to promote it, but the single 'Please' made it to number 23 in the UK despite this.

At the 2003 Grammy Awards in February, just a few weeks after Maurice's death, The Bee Gees received the Grammy Legend Award. Maurice's son Adam joined Barry and Robin in accepting Maurice's award.

Robin toured Germany, Russia and South-East Asia in 2004. His *Live* CD and DVD, recorded at the Bonn concert of his German tour – was released in 2005.

Barry reunited with Barbra Streisand to write and produce her 25th-anniversary follow-up to *Guilty*. The resulting album *Guilty Too* (released as *Guilty Pleasures* in North America) was released in September 2005 and fared well on both sides of the Atlantic.

In November 2006, Robin released another solo album, *My Favourite Carols*. It featured traditional Christmas songs and one new original composition – 'Mother Of Love'.

As part of The Bee Gees' 50th Anniversary celebrations, Barry and Robin received the Variety Club's highest accolade, the Silver Heart Tribute Award, in their hometown of Manchester in July 2009. Anniversary products included a DVD documentary titled *In Our Own Time* and a 4-CD box set titled *Mythology*, but both were delayed and were eventually released in 2010.

Robin toured Australia and New Zealand in October/November 2010 and released a DVD, *In Concert With The Danish National Concert Orchestra*, filmed in July 2009 at Ledreborg Castle in Denmark.

In November 2011, Robin was diagnosed with colorectal cancer, which had metastasised to his liver several months earlier.

Robin's classical album, *The Titanic Requiem*, co-written with his son Robin-John was made to commemorate the centenary of the sinking of the Titanic. A lavish production, it was recorded with the Royal Philharmonic Orchestra and was released in March 2012, to positive reviews. The world premiere was held at The Central Hall, Westminster, on 10 April 2012, but Robin was unable to attend due to his illness. He died in London on 20 May 2012 at the age of 62 from liver and kidney failure. His funeral was held on 8 June 2012 near his home in Thame, Oxfordshire, UK.

Understandably, Barry took the death of his third brother hard and kept a low profile for some time, but in late 2012 he announced his first-ever solo tour in Australia and New Zealand, commencing in early 2013. *The Mythology Tour* concerts celebrated the three brothers' work over the previous 50 years. The tour was a sell-out and received rave reviews from the critics.

Following the tour's success, there were further concerts in the UK and Ireland in September and October, and in the United States, beginning in May and June 2014.

Robin's final studio album, *50 St. Catherine's Drive*, was released posthumously in September 2014. Despite solid reviews, the album only reached number 70 in the UK and 39 in Germany.

Saved By the Bell – The Collected Works Of Robin Gibb: 1969-70 was a highly anticipated set released in June 2015. It included Robin's solo work from the split era and showed what a prolific writer he was. In addition, the three-CD set included *Robin's Reign* plus the legendary unreleased follow up *Sing Slowly Sisters* album and many other previously unreleased gems.

In October 2016, Barry released *In the Now*: his third solo album. The album received positive reviews worldwide and charted in the top 3 in several countries, including the UK and Australia. In the US, it peaked at number 63.

In November 2016, The Bee Gees' entire recorded catalogue was moved to Capitol Records. Fans hoped this would resume the expanded album reissue programme, but it was not to be. Instead, the label's first release was

Timeless: The All-Time Greatest Hits, which collected usual hits that had appeared on no less than seven other compilations since 2001.

A quiet period followed for Barry, although he kept himself in the public eye with a guest appearance with Coldplay at the Glastonbury Festival in 2016. The following year, he headlined the same festival on the Legends Stage.

He was awarded a knighthood in the Queen's New Year's Honours list in 2018 for services to music and charity. He formally became Sir Barry Alan Crompton Gibb on 27 June 2018 in a ceremony at Buckingham Palace officiated by Prince Charles.

In the summer of 2020, Capitol Records re-released five remasters of The Bee Gees' five albums - *Best Of Bee Gees*, *Main Course*, *Children Of The World*, *Here At Last ... Bee Gees ... Live* and *Spirits Having Flown* - on regular black vinyl and, of slightly more interest to collectors, on coloured vinyl.

In December 2020, a documentary chronicling the life and music of the Brothers Gibb – *The Bee Gees: How Can You Mend A Broken Heart* – was released. Renowned American filmmaker and producer Frank Marshall served as director for the documentary, which led its category with six Emmy Awards nominations, including Outstanding Documentary.

Hot on the heels of the documentary, Barry released *Greenfields: The Gibb Brothers Songbook, Vol. 1* in January 2021. It featured duets with various American country artists.The album topped the UK and Australian charts and ranked 15 on the US *Billboard* 200.

The Bee Gees: One For All Tour (1989)

Photo: Andrew Môn Hughes

AUSTRALIAN ALBUMS (1965-67)

THE BEE GEES SING AND PLAY 14 BARRY GIBB SONGS
(1965 Leedon)

I Was a Lover, a Leader of Men
I Don't Think It's Funny
How Love Was True
To Be or Not to Be
Timber!
Claustrophobia
Could It Be
And the Children Laughing
Wine and Women
Don't Say Goodbye
Peace of Mind
Take Hold of That Star
You Wouldn't Know
Follow the Wind

SPICKS AND SPECKS
(1966 Spin)

Monday's Rain
Many Birds
Play Down
Second Hand People
I Don't Know Why I Bother With Myself
Big Chance
Spicks and Specks
Jingle Jangle
Tint of Blue
Where Are You
Born a Man
Glass House

TURN AROUND...LOOK AT US
(1967 Festival)

Turn Around, Look At Me
The Battle Of The Blue And The Grey
The Three Kisses Of Love
Theme From Jamie McPheeters
Everyday I Have To Cry
I Want Home
Cherry Red
All Of My Life
I Am The World
I Was A Lover, A Leader Of Men
Wine And Women

AUSTRALIAN EPs

The Bee Gees EP *(Leedon)*

Wine And Women EP *(Leedon)*

Spicks And Specks EP *(Spin)*

INTERNATIONAL ALBUMS

BEE GEES 1st
(1967)

Turn of the Century
Holiday
Red Chair, Fade Away
One Minute Woman
In My Own Time
Every Christian Lion Hearted Man Will Show You
CraiseFinton Kirk Royal Academy of Arts
New York Mining Disaster 1941
Cucumber Castle
To Love Somebody
I Close My Eyes
I Can't See Nobody
Please Read Me
Close Another Door

The 2006 edition included within 'The Studio Albums 1967-1968' box set includes both mono and stereo versions of the above, plus the following bonus tracks:

Turn of the Century (Early Version)
One Minute Woman (Early Version)
Gilbert Green
New York Mining Disaster 1941 (Version One)
House of Lords
Cucumber Castle (Early Version)
Harry Braff (Early Alternate Version)
I Close My Eyes (Early Version)
I've Got to Learn
I Can't See Nobody (Alternate Take)
All Around My Clock
Mr. Wallor's Wailing Wall
CraiseFinton Kirk Royal Academy of Arts
New York Mining Disaster 1941 (Version Two)

UK
(Polydor)

UK Reissue
(RSO)

Taiwan
(CSJ)

Taiwan
(World Record)

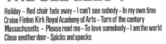

Netherlands
(Polydor – Club Edition)

Japan
(Polydor)

HORIZONTAL
(1968)

World
And the Sun Will Shine
Lemons Never Forget
Really and Sincerely
Birdie Told Me
With the Sun in My Eyes
Massachusetts
Harry Braff
Daytime Girl
The Earnest of Being George
The Change Is Made
Horizontal

The 2006 edition included within 'The Studio Albums 1967-1968' box set includes both mono and stereo versions of the above, plus the following bonus tracks:

Out of Line
Ring My Bell
Barker of the UFO
Words
Sir Geoffrey Saved the World
Sinking Ships
Really and Sincerely (Alternate version)
Swan Song (Alternate version)
Mrs. Gillespie's Refrigerator
Deeply Deeply Me
All My Christmases Came at Once
Thank You for Christmas
Silent Night/Mary's Boy Child (Medley)

'Mary's Boy Child' is incorrectly listed on the box set as 'Hark the Herald Angels Sing'.

UK

(Polydor)

USA

(ATCO)

South Africa
(Polydor)

Italy
(Polydor)

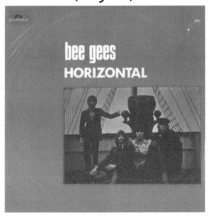

Uruguay
(Polydor)

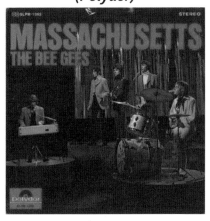

Japan
(Polydor)

RARE, PRECIOUS & BEAUTIFUL
(1968)

Where Are You?
Spicks And Specks
Play Down
Big Chance
Glass House
How Many Birds
Second Hand People
I Don't Know Why I Bother With Myself
Monday's Rain
Tint Of Blue
Jingle Jangle
Born A Man

International reissue of Australian era material

UK
(Polydor)

Canada
(Polydor)

Germany
(Karusell)

Argentina
(Karusell)

Japan
(Polydor)

USA
(ATCO)

IDEA
(1968)

Let There Be Love
Kitty Can
In The Summer of His Years
Indian Gin and Whisky Dry
Down To Earth
Such A Shame
Idea
When The Swallows Fly
I Have Decided To Join the Airforce
I Started A Joke
Kilburn Towers
Swan Song

*The US edition on the ATCO label replaced 'Such A Shame'
with 'I've Gotta Get A Message To You'.*

*The 2006 edition included within 'The Studio Albums 1967-
1968' box set includes both mono and stereo versions of the
above, plus the following bonus tracks:*

Chocolate Symphony
I've Gotta Get A Message To You (Mono single version)
Jumbo
The Singer Sang His Song
Bridges Crossing Rivers
Idea (Alternate mix)
Completely Unoriginal
Kitty Can (Alternate mix)
Come Some Christmas Eve Or Hallowe'en
Let There Be Love (Alternate mix)
Gena's Theme
Another Cold And Windy Day
Sitting In The Meadow

UK
(Polydor)

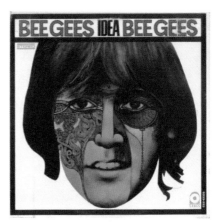

USA
(ATCO)

Canada
(Polydor)

Uruguay
(Polydor)

Netherlands
(Polydor – Club Edition)

Germany
(Polydor – Club Edition)

RARE, PRECIOUS & BEAUTIFUL – VOLUME 2
(1968)

I Was A Lover, A Leader Of Men
Follow The Wind
Claustrophobia
Theme From The Travels Of Jaimie McPheeters
Every Day I Have To Cry
Take Hold O That Star
Could It Be
To Be Or Not To Be
The Three Kisses Of Love
Cherry Red
All Of My Life
Don't Say Goodbye

International reissue of Australian era material

UK
(Polydor)

Australia
(Festival)

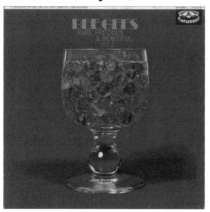

Germany
(Karusell)

France
(Triumph)

Japan
(Polydor)

USA
(ATCO)

RARE, PRECIOUS & BEAUTIFUL – VOLUME 3
(1969)

Wine And Women
I Don't Think It's Funny
Turn Around, Look At Me
I Am The World
The Battle Of The Battle Of The Blue And The Grey
How Love Was True
And The Children Laughing
You Wouldn't Know
I Want Home
Timber!
I Was A Lover, A Leader Of Men
Peace Of Mind

International reissue of Australian era material

UK
(Polydor)

Australia
(Festival)

Germany
(Karusell)

France
(Triumph)

Japan
(Polydor)

ODESSA
(1969)

Odessa (City On The Black Sea)
You'll Never See My Face Again
Black Diamond
Marley Purt Drive
Edison
Melody Fair
Suddenly
Whisper Whisper
Lamplight
Sound Of Love
Give Your Best
Seven Seas Symphony
With All Nations (International Anthem)
I Laugh In Your Face
Never Say Never Again
First Of May
The British Opera

The 2009 edition includes both mono and stereo versions of the above, plus a bonus disc called 'Sketches For Odessa' containing the following bonus tracks:

Odessa (Demo)
You'll Never See My Face Again" (Alternate Mix)
Black Diamond (Demo)
Marley Purt Drive (Alternate Mix)
Barbara Came To Stay
Edison (Alternate Mix)
Melody Fair (Demo)
Melody Fair (Alternate Mix)
Suddenly (Alternate Mix)
Whisper Whisper – Part Two (Alternate Version)
Lamplight (Demo)
Lamplight (Alternate Version)
Sound Of Love (Alternate Mix)
Give Your Best (Alternate Mix)
Seven Seas Symphony (Demo)
With All Nations (International Anthem) (Vocal Version)

UK
(Polydor)

France
(RSO - Reissue)

Argentina (Volume 1)
(Polydor)

Argentina (Volume 2)
(Polydor)

Argentina (Volume 1)
(RSO - Reissue)

Argentina (Volume 2)
(RSO - Reissue)

BEST OF BEE GEES
(1969)

Holiday
I've Gotta Get A Message To You
I Can't See Nobody
Words
I Started A Joke
Spicks And Specks
First of May
World
Massachusetts
To Love Somebody
Every Christian Lion Hearted Man Will Show You
New York Mining Disaster 1941

2020 Capitol/UMe Reissue
Berry Coloured Vinyl

UK
(Polydor)

Spain
(Polydor)

Greece
(Polydor)

ROBIN GIBB

ROBIN'S REIGN

(1970)

August October
Gone GoneGone
The Worst Girl In This Town
Give Me A Smile
Down Came The Sun
Mother And Jack
Saved By The Bell
Weekend
Farmer Ferdinand Hudson
Lord Bless All
Most Of My Life

German edition includes 'One Million Years'

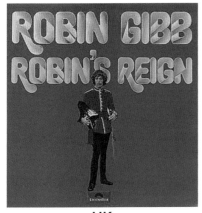

UK
(Polydor)

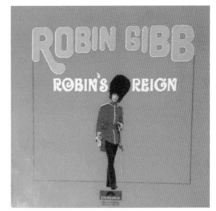

Austria
(Polydor – Club Edition)

Japan
(Polydor)

Germany
(Spectrum – Reissue CD)

ROBIN GIBB
CUCUMBER CASTLE
(1970)

If Only I Had My Mind On Something Else
I.O.I.O.
Then You Left Me
The Lord
I Was The Child
I Lay Down And Die
Sweetheart
Bury Me Down By The River
My Thing
The Chance Of Love
Turning Tide
Don't Forget To Remember

UK
(Polydor)

Germany
(Polydor – Club Edition)

Greece
(Polydor)

MAURICE GIBB
Railroad/I've Come Back
(1970)

Germany **Singapore** **Italy**
(Polydor) **(Polydor)** **(Polydor)**

From Maurice's unreleased solo album 'The Loner'

BARRY GIBB
I'll Kiss Your Memory/This Time
(1970)

Germany **France** **Spain**
(Polydor) **(Polydor)** **(Polydor)**

From Barry's unreleased solo album 'The Kid's No Good'

MAURICE GIBB
SING A RUDE SONG
(1970)

I'm In A Mood To Get My Teeth Into A Song
That's What They Say
This Time It's Happiness
Whoops Cockie!
It Was Only A Friendly Kiss
Whoops Cockie! (Reprise) / We've Been And Gone And Done
It *
Haven't The Words
You Don't Know What It's Like To Fall In Love At Forty
Waiting On The Off Chance
Waiting For The Royal Train *
I'm Nobody In Particular
Wave Goodbye
Leave Me Here To Linger With The Ladies *
The One And Only
Sing A Rude Song *

*The entire album was produced by Mauriceand he performs on
the songs noted **

INCEPTION/NOSTALGIA
(1970)

In The Morning
Like Nobody Else
Daydream
Lonely Winter
You're The Reason
Coalman
Butterfly
Storm
Lum-De-Loo
You're Nobody Till Somebody Loves You
You Won't See Me
The End
I'll Know What To Do
All By Myself
Ticket To Ride
I Love You Because
Paperback Writer
Somewhere
The Twelfth Of Never
Forever
Top Hat
Hallelujah, I Love Her So
Terrible Way To Treat Your Baby
Exit Stage Right

First release of previously unreleased Australian era material

Germany
(Karusell)

France
(Triumph)

Japan
(Polydor)

2 YEARS ON
(1970)

2 Years On
Portrait Of Louise
Man For All Seasons
Sincere Relation
Back Home
The 1st Mistake I Made
Lonely Days
Alone Again
Tell Me Why
Lay It On Me
Every Second, Every Minute
I'm Weeping

Germany
(Polydor)

Australia
(Spin)

New Zealand
(Spin)

Greece
(Polydor)

Germany
(Polydor – Club Edition)

Brazil
(Polydor)

MELODY
(1971)

In The Morning *
In The Morning (Reprise) **
Melody Fair *
Melody Fair (Reprise) **
Spicks & Specks **
Romance Theme In F **
Give Your Best *
To Love Somebody *
Working On It Night And Day **
First Of May *
First Of May (Reprise) **
Seaside Banjo *
Teachers Chase *
Teach Your Children ***

* - The Bee Gees
** - Richard Hewson Orchestra
*** - Crosby, Stills, Nash & Young

UK
(Polydor)

UK
(Polydor)

USA
(ATCO)

France
(Polydor)

Japan
(Polydor – Club Edition)

Uruguay
(Polydor)

TRAFALGAR
(1971 Polydor/Atco)

How Can You Mend a Broken Heart
Israel
The Greatest Man in the World
It's Just the Way
Remembering
Somebody Stop the Music
Trafalgar
Don't Wanna Live Inside Myself
When Do I
Dearest
Lion in Winter
Walking Back to Waterloo

UK
(Polydor)

USA
(Mobile Fidelity Sound Labs)

TO WHOM IT MAY CONCERN
(1972 Polydor/Atco)

Run to Me
We Lost the Road
Never Been Alone
Paper Mache, Cabbages and Kings
I Can Bring Love
I Held a Party
Please Don't Turn Out the Lights
Sea of Smiling Faces
Bad Bad Dreams
You Know It's for You
Alive
Road to Alaska
Sweet Song of Summer

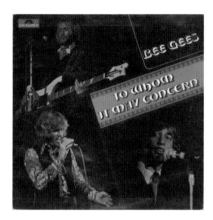

UK
(Polydor)

Venezuela
(Polydor)

Australia – inner gatefold
(Spin)

MASSACHUSETTS
(1972Contour)

Massachusetts
Tomorrow Tomorrow
Sir Geoffrey Saved The World
Sinking Ships
Sweetheart
The Singer Sang His Song
New York Mining Disaster 1941
Lamplight
On Time
Barker Of The U.F.O.
Close Another Door
The Lord

UK
(1972)

UK - Reissue
(1978 Contour)

UK - Reissue
(1983 Contour)

LIFE IN A TIN CAN
(1973 RSO)

Saw a New Morning
I Don't Wanna Be the One
South Dakota Morning
Living in Chicago
While I Play
My Life Has Been a Song
Come Home Johnny Bridie
Method to My Madness

UK
(Polydor)

Australia
(RSO)

Malaysia
(No record label stated)

BEST OF BEE GEES VOL. 2
(1973 RSO)

UK Track Listing
How Can You Mend A Broken Heart
I.O.I.O.
Don't Wanna Live Inside Myself
Melody Fair
My World
Let There Be Love
Saved By The Bell
Lonely Days
Morning Of My Life
Don't Forget To Remember
And The Sun Will Shine
Run To Me
Man For All Seasons
Alive

US Track Listing
Wouldn't I Be Someone
I.O.I.O.
My World
Saved By The Bell
Don't Forget To Remember
And The Sun Will Shine
Run To Me
Man For All Seasons
How Can You Mend A Broken Heart
Don't Wanna Live Inside Myself
Melody Fair
Let There Be Love
Lonely Days
Morning Of My Life
Alive

UK
(RSO)

USA
(RSO)

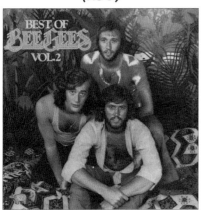

Australia
(RSO)

South Africa
(RSO)

MR.NATURAL
(1974 RSO)

Charade
Throw a Penny
Down the Road
Voices
Give a Hand, Take a Hand
Dogs
Mr. Natural
Lost in Your Love
I Can't Let You Go
Heavy Breathing
Had a Lot of Love Last Night

UK
(1974 Contour)

UK - Reissue
(1978 Contour)

GOTTA GET A MESSAGE TO YOU
(1974 Contour)

I'veGotta Get A Message To You
Elisa
Road To Alaska
My Life Has Been A Songs
Jumbo
I Am The World
World
Railroad
One Million Years
I'll Kiss Your Memory
It Doesn't Matter Much To Me
Paper Mache, Cabbages And Kings

MAIN COURSE
(1975 RSO)

Nights On Broadway
Jive Talkin'
Wind of Change
Songbird
Fanny (Be Tender with My Love)
All This Making Love
Country Lanes
Come On Over
Edge Of the Universe
Baby As You Turn Away

2020 Capitol/UMe Reissue
Whitewater Vinyl

USA
(RSO)

Germany
(RSO)

Greece
(RSO)

Russia
(Melodiya)

Russia
(Melodiya – Coloured Vinyl Editions)

CHILDREN OF THE WORLD
(1976 RSO)

You Should Be Dancing
You Stepped Into My Life
Love So Right
Lovers
Can't Keep A Good Man Down
Boogie Child
Love Me
Subway
The Way It Was
Children Of The World

2020 Capitol/UMe Reissue
Sunshine Yellow Vinyl

UK
(Riva)

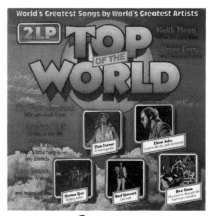

Germany
(RSO)

Greece
(RSO)

Russia
(Melodiya)

ALL THIS AND WORLD WAR II
(1976)

Golden Slumbers/Carry That Weight
She Came In Through The Bathroom Window
Sun King

HERE AT LAST ... BEE GEES ... LIVE
(1977 RSO)

I've Gotta Get A Message to You
Love So Right
Edge Of The Universe
Come On Over
Can't Keep A Good Man Down
New York Mining Disaster 1941
Run To Me
World
Holiday
I Can't See Nobody
I Started A Joke
Massachusetts
How Can You Mend A Broken Heart
To Love Somebody
You Should Be Dancing
Boogie Child
Down The Road
Words
Wind Of Change
Nights On Broadway
Jive Talkin'
Lonely Days

2020 Capitol/UMe Reissue
Tangerine Vinyl

Australia **(RSO – Platinum** **Vinyl)**	**South Africa** **(RSO – Orange Vinyl)**	**UK** **(RSO – Red Vinyl)**

SATURDAY NIGHT FEVER
(1977 RSO)

Stayin' Alive
How Deep Is Your Love
Night Fever
More Than A Woman
Jive Talkin'
You Should Be Dancing

SGT.PEPPER'S LONELY HEARTS CLUB BAND
(1978 A&M / RSO)

Sgt. Pepper's Lonely Hearts Club Band (The Bee Gees and Paul Nicholas)
With a Little Help from My Friends (Peter Frampton and The Bee Gees)
Here Comes the Sun (Sandy Farina)
Getting Better (Peter Frampton and The Bee Gees)
Lucy in the Sky with Diamonds (Dianne Steinberg and Stargard)
I Want You (She's So Heavy) (The Bee Gees, Dianne Steinberg, Paul Nicholas, Donald Pleasence, Stargard)

Good Morning Good Morning (Paul Nicholas, Peter Frampton and The Bee Gees)
She's Leaving Home" (The Bee Gees, Jay MacIntosh and John Wheeler)
You Never Give Me Your Money (Paul Nicholas and Dianne Steinberg)
Oh! Darling (Robin Gibb)
Maxwell's Silver Hammer (Steve Martin)
Polythene Pam (The Bee Gees)
She Came in Through the Bathroom Window (The Bee Gees)
Nowhere Man (The Bee Gees)
Sgt. Pepper's Lonely Hearts Club Band (Reprise) (Peter Frampton and The Bee Gees)

Got to Get You into My Life (Earth, Wind & Fire)
Strawberry Fields Forever (Sandy Farina)
When I'm Sixty-Four (Frankie Howerd and Sandy Farina)
Mean Mr. Mustard (Frankie Howerd)
Fixing a Hole (George Burns)
Because (Alice Cooper and The Bee Gees)
Golden Slumbers (Peter Frampton)
Carry That Weight (The Bee Gees)

Come Together (Aerosmith)
Being for the Benefit of Mr. Kite (Peter Frampton, The Bee Gees, and George Burns)
The Long and Winding Road (Peter Frampton)
A Day in the Life (Barry Gibb and The Bee Gees)
Get Back (Billy Preston)
Sgt. Pepper's Lonely Hearts Club Band (Finale) (Full cast)

UK
(A&M – Pink Vinyl)

Birth Of Brilliance
(Infinity 1978)

Wine And Woman
I Was A Lover, A Leader Of Men
Timber!
Claustrophobia
Could It Be
Peace Of Mind
To Be Or Not To Be
I Don't Think It's Funny
Three Kisses Of Love
The Battle Of The Blue And The Grey
Theme From Jaimie McPheeters
Turn Around, Look At Me
Every Day I Have To Cry
How Love Was True
You Won't See Me
Lonely Winter
In The Morning
Like Nobody Else
All By Myself
Storm
Butterfly
Terrible Way To Treat Your Baby
Exit, Stage Right
Coalman
I Am The World
Cherry Red

I Want Home
Monday's Rain
How Many Birds
Secondhand People
Born A Man
Spicks & Specks

SPIRITS HAVING FLOWN
(1979)

Tragedy
Too Much Heaven
Love You Inside Out
Reaching Out
Spirits (Having Flown)
Search, Find
Stop (Think Again)
Living Together
I'm Satisfied
Until

2020 Capitol/UMe Reissue
Blood Red Vinyl

UK
(Polydor)

UK
(Polydor)

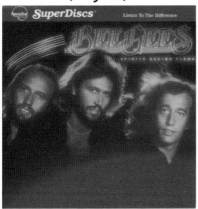

USA
(Nautilus)

USSR
(Melodiya)

Argentina
(Polydor)

Taiwan
(Liming Record)

BEE GEES GREATEST
(1979 RSO)

Jive Talkin'
Night Fever
Tragedy
You Should Be Dancing
Stayin' Alive
How Deep Is Your Love
Love So Right
Too Much Heaven
(Our Love) Don't Throw It All Away
Fanny (Be Tender with My Love)
If I Can't Have You
You Stepped Into My Life
Love Me
More Than a Woman
Rest Your Love on Me
Nights on Broadway
Spirits (Having Flown)
Love You Inside Out
Wind of Change
Children of the World

LIVING EYES
(1981 RSO)

Living Eyes
He's A Liar
Paradise
Don't Fall In Love With Me
Soldiers
I Still Love You
Wildflower
Nothing Could Be Good
Cryin' Every Day
Be Who You Are

ROBIN GIBB
HOW OLD ARE YOU?
(1983 Polydor)

Juliet
How Old Are You
In and Out of Love
Kathy's Gone
Don't Stop the Night
Another Lonely Night in New York
Danger
He Can't Love You
Hearts on Fire
I Believe in Miracles

STAYING ALIVE
(1983 RSO)

The Woman in You
I Love You Too Much
Breakout
Someone Belonging to Someone
Life Goes On
Stayin' Alive (edited version)

ROBIN GIBB
SECRET AGENT
(1984 Polydor)

Boys Do Fall in Love
In Your Diary
Robot
Rebecca
Secret Agent
Living in Another World
X-Ray Eyes
King of Fools
Diamonds

BARRY GIBB
NOW VOYAGER
(1984 Polydor)

I Am Your Driver
Fine Line
Face to Face
Shatterproof
Shine, Shine
Lesson in Love
One Night (For Lovers)
Stay Alone
Temptation
She Says
The Hunter

MAURICE GIBB
A BREED APART
(1984)

Hold Her In Your Hand
A Breed Apart
Jim's Theme
Solitude
The Intruders
On Time
Mike And The Mountain
Adam's Dream
A Touch Apart
The Breed Ending
Hold Her In Your Hand (Instrumental)

*Movie soundtrack – the only songs released on record were
Hold Her In Your Hand/Hold Her In Your Hand (Instrumental)*

ROBIN GIBB
WALLS HAVE EYES
(1985 Polydor)

European Track Listing
You Don't Say Us Anymore
Like a Fool
Heartbeat in Exile
Remedy
Toys
Someone to Believe In
Gone with the Wind
These Walls Have Eyes
Possession
Do You Love Her?

US Track Listing
Someone to Believe In
Like a Fool
Gone with the Wind
Toys
These Walls Have Eyes
Do You Love Her?
Possession
Heartbeat in Exile
You Don't Say Us Anymore
Remedy

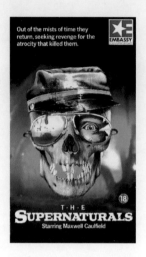

MAURICE GIBB
THE SUPERNATURALS
(1986)

Movie soundtrack – no song titles available as the score exists merely titled 'The Supernaturals'.

Commercial issues on VHS do not feature Maurice's score – his was limited to broadcasts on cable and satellite TV

He also makes a cameo appearance in the movie

E.S.P.
(1987 Warner Brothers)

E.S.P.
You Win Again
Live or Die (Hold Me Like A Child)
Giving Up The Ghost
The Longest Night
This Is Your Life
Angela
Overnight
Crazy For Your Love
Backtafunk
E.S.P. (Reprise)

The Warner Bros. Years bonus tracks
E.S.P. (Demo Version)
Angela (Edit)
E.S.P" (Edit)
You Win Again (Extended Version)
E.S.P. (Extended Version)

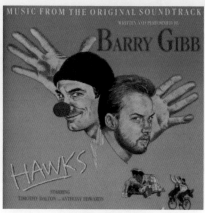

Netherlands
(Polydor)

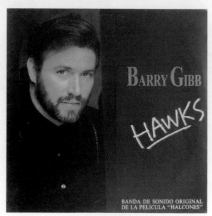

Argentina
(Polydor)

BARRY GIBB
HAWKS
(1988 Polydor)

System of Love
Childhood Days
Moonlight Madness
My Eternal Love
Where Tomorrow Is
Celebration de la Vie
Chain Reaction (performed by Diana Ross)
Cover You
Not in Love at All
Letting Go

ONE
(1989 Warner Brothers)

Ordinary Lives
One
Bodyguard
It's My Neighborhood
Tears
Tokyo Nights
Flesh And Blood
Wish You Were Here
House Of Shame
Will You Ever Let Me
Wing And A Prayer

The Warner Bros. Years bonus tracks
Shape Of Things To Come
One" (Edit)
One" (12" Dance Version)
One (12" Club Mix)

TALES FROM THE BROTHERS GIBB|
(1990 Polydor) (4CD box)

Disc 1 - Chapter I: 1967–1970

New York Mining Disaster 1941
I Can't See Nobody
To Love Somebody
Holiday
Massachusetts
Barker of the U.F.O.
World
Sir Geoffrey Saved the World
And the Sun Will Shine
Words
Sinking Ships
Jumbo
The Singer Sang His Song
I've Gotta Get a Message to You
I Started a Joke
First of May
Melody Fair
Tomorrow Tomorrow
Sun in My Morning
Saved by the Bell (Robin Gibb)
Don't Forget to Remember
If I Only Had My Mind on
Something Else
I.O.I.O.
Railroad (Maurice Gibb)
I'll Kiss Your Memory (Barry Gibb)

Disc 2 - Chapter II: 1971–1974

Lonely Days
Morning of My Life (In the Morning)
How Can You Mend a Broken Heart
Country Woman
Don't Wanna Live Inside Myself
My World
On Time
Run to Me
Alive
Saw a New Morning
Wouldn't I Be Someone
Elisa
King and Country
Mr. Natural
It Doesn't Matter Much to Me
Throw a Penny
Charade

Disc 3 - Chapter III: 1975–1979	Disc 4 - Chapter IV: 1981–1989
Jive Talkin'	
Nights on Broadway	He's a Liar
Fanny (Be Tender with My Love)	Another Lonely Night in New York (Robin Gibb)
You Should Be Dancing	The Woman in You
Love So Right	Someone Belonging to Someone
Boogie Child	
Edge of the Universe"(Live)	Toys (Robin Gibb)
How Deep Is Your Love	My Eternal Love (Barry Gibb)
Stayin' Alive	Where Tomorrow Is (Barry Gibb)
Night Fever	
More Than a Woman	Letting Go (Barry Gibb)
If I Can't Have You	E.S.P. (Demo Version)
(Our Love) Don't Throw It All Away	You Win Again
	Ordinary Lives
Too Much Heaven	One
Tragedy	Juliet (Live)
Love You Inside Out	To Love Somebody (Live)
	Medley: (Live
	New York Mining Disaster 1941
	Holiday
	Too Much Heaven
	Heartbreaker
	Islands In The Stream
	Run To Me
	World
	Spicks and Specks (Live)

The three Barry Gibb solo tracks on Disc 4 were omitted from the North American release.

Reissue in book style case

THE VERY BEST OF THE BEE GEES
(1990 Polydor)

New York Mining Disaster 1941
To Love Somebody
Massachusetts
World
Words
I've Gotta Get a Message to You
First of May
Don't Forget to Remember
Saved by the Bell
Run to Me
Jive Talkin'
Nights on Broadway
You Should Be Dancing
How Deep Is Your Love
More Than a Woman
Stayin' Alive
Night Fever
Too Much Heaven
Tragedy
You Win Again
Ordinary Lives

HIGH CIVILIZATION
(1991 Warner Brothers)

High Civilization
Secret Love
When He's Gone
Happy Ever After
Party With No Name
Ghost Train
Dimensions
The Only Love
Human Sacrifice
True Confessions
Evolution

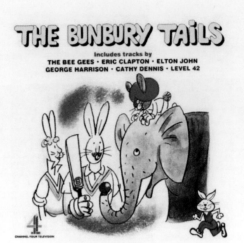

BUNBURY TAILS
(1992 Polydor)

We're The Bunbury's (The Bee Gees)
Bunbury Afternoon (The Bee Gees)
Eyes (Kelli Wolfe)
Fight (No Matter How Long) (Eric Clapton & The Bee Gees)
Up The Revolution (Elton John)
Seasons (No Hat Moon)

All songs noted are written by The Bee Gee Gees and apart from 'Up The Revolution', include them in instrumental, vocal and production capacities

UK
(Riva)

Guatemala
(Dideca International)

SIZE ISN'T EVERYTHING
(1993 Polydor)

Paying The Price Of Love
Kiss Of Life
How To Fall In Love, Part 1
Omega Man
Haunted House
Heart Like Mine
Anything For You
Blue Island
Above And Beyond
For Whom The Bell Tolls
Fallen Angel
Decadance

The US edition omits 'Decadance'

STILL WATERS
(1997 Polydor)

Alone
I Surrender
I Could Not Love You More
Still Waters Run Deep
My Lover's Prayer
With My Eyes Closed
Irresistible Force
Closer Than Close
I Will
Obsessions
Miracles Happen
Smoke and Mirrors

Bonus tracks
Rings Around the Moon
Love Never Dies

VH1 STORYTELLERS
(1997 Polydor)

Words
I Started A Joke
Jive Talkin'
I've Gotta Get A Message To You
To Love Somebody

ONE NIGHT ONLY
(1998 Polydor)

Intro: You Should Be Dancing/Alone
Massachusetts
To Love Somebody
Words
Closer Than Close
Islands In The Stream
(Our Love) Don't Throw It All Away (featuring Andy Gibb)
Night Fever/More Than A Woman
Lonely Days
New York Mining Disaster 1941
I Can't See Nobody
And The Sun Will Shine
Nights On Broadway
How Can You Mend A Broken Heart
Heartbreaker
Guilty
Immortality (featuring Celine Dion)
Tragedy
I Started A Joke
Grease (featuring Frankie Valli)
Jive Talkin'
How Deep Is Your Love
Stayin' Alive
You Should Be Dancing

Reissue bonus CD

THE LIMITED EDITION 6 TRACK CD
(1999 Polydor)

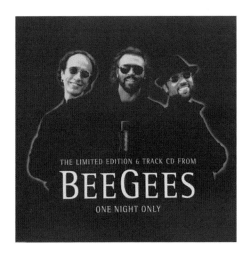

I've Gotta Get A Message to You
One
Still Waters (Run Deep)
Morning Of My Life (In the Morning)
Too Much Heaven
Run To Me

BRILLIANT FROM BIRTH
(Spin 1998)

Disc 1

The Battle Of The Blue And The Grey
The Three Kisses Of Love
Timber
Take Hold Of That Star
Peace Of Mind
Don't Say Goodbye
Claustrophobia
Could It Be
Turn Around, Look At Me
Theme From Jaimie McPheeters
Everyday I Have To Cry
You Wouldn't Know
Wine And Women
Follow The Wind
I Was A Lover, A Leader Of Men
And The Children Laughing

I Don't Think It's Funny
How Love Was True
To Be Or Not To Be
Cherry Red
I Want Home
The End
Hallelujah, I Love Her So
I Love You Because
Somewhere
The Twelfth Of Never
You're The Reason
You're Nobody 'Til Somebody Loves You
All By Myself
Butterfly
Can't You See That She's Mine
From Me To You

Disc 2

Monday's Rain
All Of My Life
Where Are You
Playdown
Big Chance
Glass House
How Many Birds
Second Hand People
I Don't Know Why I Bother With Myself
Jingle Jangle
Tint Of Blue
Born A Man
Spicks & Specks
I Am The World
Daydream
Forever

Coalman
Exit Stage Right
Paperback Writer
I'll Know What To Do
In The Morning
Like Nobody Else
Lonely Winter
Lum-Dee-Loo
Storm
Terrible Way To Treat Your Baby
Yesterday's Gone
You Won't See Me
Top Hat
Just One Look
Ticket To Ride

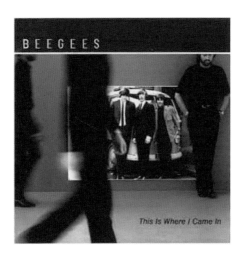

THIS IS WHERE I CAME IN
(2001 Polydor)

This Is Where I Came In
She Keeps On
Wedding Day
Man In The Middle
Déjà Vu
Technicolor Dreams
Walking On Air
Loose Talk Costs Lives
Embrace
The Extra Mile
Voice In The Wilderness

UK/Japan/Australia bonus tracks
Just In Case
Promise The Earth

US Target Stores special edition contained a second CD containing three songs performed live for VH1 Storytellers in 1996

I've Gotta Get A Message To You
Run To Me
Too Much Heaven

THEIR GREATEST HITS: THE RECORD
(2001 Polydor)

New York Mining Disaster 1941
To Love Somebody
Holiday
Massachusetts
World
Words
I've Gotta Get a Message to You
I Started a Joke
First of May
Jumbo
Saved By the Bell
Don't Forget to Remember
Lonely Days
How Can You Mend a Broken Heart
My World
Run to Me
Jive Talkin'
Nights on Broadway
Fanny (Be Tender with My Love)
Love So Right
If I Can't Have You
Love Me
You Should Be Dancing
Stayin' Alive
How Deep Is Your Love

Night Fever
More Than a Woman
Emotion
Too Much Heaven
Tragedy
Love You Inside Out
Guilty (Barbra Streisand and Barry Gibb)
Heartbreaker
Islands in the Stream
You Win Again
One
Secret Love
For Whom the Bell Tolls
Alone
Immortality (Demo version)
This Is Where I Came In
Spicks and Specks

Copies sold at the American retailer Target included a bonus disc entitled 5 Live Recordings.

Massachusetts
To Love Somebody
Jive Talkin'
How Can You Mend A Broken Heart
How Deep Is Your Love

Germany
(SPV)

Germany – Reissue
(111 Records)

ROBIN GIBB
MAGNET
(2002)

Please
Don't Wanna Wait Forever
Wish You Were Here
No Doubt
Special
Inseparable
Don't Rush
Watching You
Earth Angel
Another Lonely Night in New York
Love Hurts

UK
(Polydor)

USA
(Universal)

NUMBER ONES
(2004)

Massachusetts
World
Words
I've Gotta Get a Message to You
I Started a Joke
Don't Forget to Remember
How Can You Mend a Broken Heart
Jive Talkin'
You Should Be Dancing
How Deep Is Your Love
Stayin' Alive
Night Fever
Too Much Heaven
Tragedy
More Than a Woman
Love You Inside Out
You Win Again
Man in the Middle
Bonus tracks
Islands in the Stream
Immortality" (original demo version)

The US edition omits 'More Than A Woman' and the two UK bonus tracks but includes 'Lonely Days' 'Love So Right'.
The special edition included a five track DVD featuring: 'How Can You Mend A Broken Heart'; 'How Deep Is Your Love'; 'Jive Talkin''; Massachusetts' and 'I Started A Joke' from the television special, 'An Audience With The Bee Gees'.

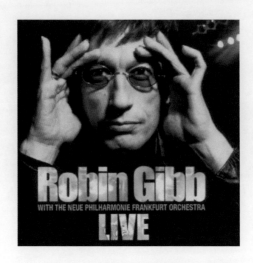

ROBIN GIBB
LIVE (WITH THE NEUE PHILHARMONIE ORCHESTRA)
(2005)

Night Fever
I've Gotta Get A Message To You
How Deep Is Your Love
Nights On Broadway
Love Hurts
Massachusetts
My Lover's Prayer
New York Mining Disaster 1941
Please
Saved By The Bell
To Love Somebody
Words
You Win Again
Juliet
Tragedy
Jive Talkin'
Stayin' Alive

LOVE SONGS
(2006 Polydor)

To Love Somebody
Words
First of May
Lonely Days
How Can You Mend a Broken Heart
How Deep Is Your Love
More Than a Woman
(Our Love) Don't Throw It All Away
Emotion
Too Much Heaven
Heartbreaker
Islands in the Stream (Live)
Juliet
Secret Love
For Whom the Bell Tolls
Heart Like Mine *
Closer Than Close
I Could Not Love You More
Wedding Day
Bonus track
Lovers and Friends (featuring Ronan Keating)

BARRY GIBB

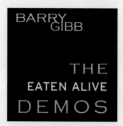

THE EATEN ALIVE DEMOS
(2006 iTunes Download only)

Oh, Teacher
Experience
More And More
I'm Watching You
Love On The Line
(I Love) Being In Love With You
Crime Of Passion
Don't Give Up On Each Other

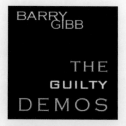

THE GUILTY DEMOS
(2006 iTunes Download only)

Guilty
Woman In Love
Run Wild
Promises
The Love Inside
What Kind Of Fool
Life Story
Make It Like A Memory
Carried Away
Secrets

THE EYES THAT SEE IN THE DARK DEMOS
(2006 iTunes Download only)

This Woman
You And I
Buried Treasure
Islands In The Stream
Living With You
Evening Star
Hold Me
Midsummer Nights
I Will Always Love You
Eyes That See In The Dark

THE HEARTBREAKER DEMOS
(2006 iTunes Download only)

Heartbreaker
It Makes No Difference
Yours
Take The Short Way Home
Misunderstood
All The Love In The World
I Can't See Anything (But You)
Just One More Night
You Are My Love

THE STUDIO ALBUMS 1967-1968
(2006 Reprise)

Box set includes both the mono and stereo versions of 'Bee Gees 1ˢᵗ' 'Horizontal' and 'Idea', plus bonus tracks as detailed on the entries for the original albums.

ROBIN GIBB
MY FAVOURITE CAROLS
(2006)

Mother of Love
In the Bleak Midwinter
Silent Night
God Rest Ye Merry, Gentlemen
Good King Wenceslas
Away in a Manger
Once in Royal David's City
I Saw Three Ships
Hark! The Herald Angels Sing
Come Some Christmas Eve Or Halloween
Ellan Vannin
In the Bleak Midwinter/O Come All Ye Faithful/Hark! The Herald
Angels Sing/While Shepherds Watched Their Flocks

The track-listing above is for the German edition.

*The Hong Kong release omits 'Come Some Christmas Eve Or
Halloween' and 'Ellan Vannin' while the US edition omits these
tracks and 'Mother Of Love'.*

*All versions included a ten-minute video: 'A Personal Christmas
Moment with Robin Gibb'. The German edition incuded it as a
CD-ROM element on the CD, while the US and Hong Kong
editions included it on a separate DVD.*

Germany
(Edel)

USA
(Koch)

Hong Kong
(Evosound)

BEE GEES GREATEST
(2007 Rhino)

*This two CD reissue includes all the songs on the original 1979
release plus the following bonus tracks:*

Warm Ride
Stayin' Alive (Promo 12" version)
You Should Be Dancing (Jason Bentley/Philip Steir remix)
If I Can't Have You (Count Da Money remix)
Night Fever (GRN remix)
How Deep Is Your Love (Supreme Beings of Leisure remix)
Stayin' Alive (Teddybears remix)
If I Can't Have You (The Disco Boys remix)

ODESSA
(2009 Reprise)

This three CD edition includes both mono and stereo versions of the original 1969 album release, plus a bonus disc called 'Sketches For Odessa' containing the following bonus tracks:

Odessa (Demo)
You'll Never See My Face Again (Alternate Mix)
Black Diamond (Demo)
Marley Purt Drive (Alternate Mix)
Barbara Came To Stay
Edison (Alternate Mix)
Melody Fair (Demo)
Melody Fair (Alternate Mix)
Suddenly (Alternate Mix)
Whisper Whisper – Part Two (Alternate Version)
Lamplight (Demo)
Lamplight (Alternate Version)
Sound Of Love (Alternate Mix)
Give Your Best (Alternate Mix)
Seven Seas Symphony (Demo)
With All Nations (International Anthem) (Vocal Version)

THE ULTIMATE BEE GEES
(2009 Polydor)

You Should Be Dancing
Stayin' Alive
Jive Talkin'
Nights on Broadway
Tragedy
Night Fever
More Than a Woman
Fanny (Be Tender with My Love)
Spirits (Having Flown)
If I Can't Have You
Boogie Child
Love You Inside Out
You Win Again
One
Secret Love
Alone
Still Waters (Run Deep)
This Is Where I Came In
Spicks and Specks"(Live)
How Deep Is Your Love
To Love Somebody
Words
How Can You Mend a Broken Heart
Too Much Heaven
Emotion
Lonely Days

Run to Me
Love So Right
For Whom the Bell Tolls
I've Gotta Get a Message to You
New York Mining Disaster 1941
Massachusetts
I Started a Joke
World
First of May
Holiday
Don't Forget to Remember
Islands in the Stream
Heartbreaker"(Live)
Guilty" (Live)

Bonus track on Japanese edition - 'Melody Fair'

*The Deluxe Edition included a bonus DVD containing
promotional clips and videos*

Spicks and Specks
New York Mining Disaster 1941
Massachusetts
I've Gotta Get a Message to You
Tomorrow, Tomorrow
Lonely Days
How Can You Mend a Broken Heart
Run to Me
Jive Talkin'
Night Fever
Stayin' Alive
How Deep Is Your Love
Too Much Heaven
For Whom the Bell Tolls
Alone
Still Waters (Run Deep)
You Win Again
One

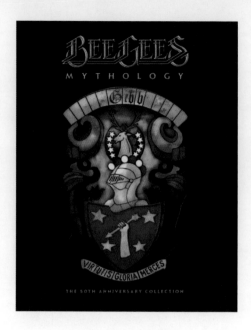

MYTHOLOGY
(2010 Reprise)

Disc 1 – Barry

Spirits (Having Flown)	Don't Forget to Remember
You Win Again	If I Can't Have You
To Love Somebody	Alone
Tragedy	Heartbreaker
Too Much Heaven	How Deep Is Your Love
First of May	Love You Inside Out
More Than a Woman	Stayin' Alive
Love So Right	Barker of the UFO
Night Fever	Swan Song
Words	Spicks and Specks

Disc 2 – Robin

I Am the World	Saved by the Bell
New York Mining Disaster 1941	My World
I Can't See Nobody	Run to Me
Holiday	Love Me
Massachusetts	Juliet
Sir Geoffrey Saved the World	The Longest Night
And the Sun Will Shine	Fallen Angel
The Singer Sang His Song	Rings Around the Moon
I've Gotta Get a Message to You	Embrace
I Started a Joke	Islands in the Stream
Odessa (City on the Black Sea)	

Disc 3 – Maurice

Man in the Middle	Omega Man
Closer Than Close	Walking on Air
Dimensions	Country Woman
House of Shame	Angel of Mercy (with Samantha Gibb)
Suddenly	Above and Beyond
Railroad	Hold Her in Your Hand
Overnight	You Know It's for You
It's Just the Way	Wildflower
Lay It on Me	On Time
Trafalgar	The Bridge (with Adam & Samantha Gibb)

Disc 4 – Andy

Shadow Dancing	Time Is Time
I Just Want to Be Your Everything	Me (Without You)
(Love Is) Thicker Than Water	After Dark
An Everlasting Love	Warm Ride
Desire	Too Many Looks in Your Eyes
(Our Love) Don't Throw it All Away	Man on Fire (Demo)
Flowing Rivers	Arrow Through the Heart (Demo)
Words and Music	Starlight
I Can't Help It (Duet with Olivia Newton-John)	Dance to the Light of the Morning
	In the End

Reissue in fatbox and slipcase

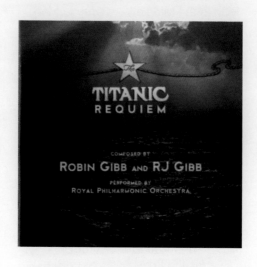

ROBIN GIBB & RJ GIBB
Performed by the ROYAL PHILHARMONIC ORCHESTRA
(2012 Rhino)

Triumph (Shipbuilding)
Farewell (The Immigrant Song)
Maiden Voyage
New York Suite In C Major
Sub Astris (Under The Stars)
Kyrie
SOS (Tract)
Distress (Confutatis)
Salvation (Gradual)
Reflections
Daybreak
Christmas Day
Libera Me
Don't Cry Alone
In Paradise (Awakening)

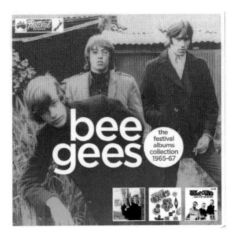

**The Bee Gees Sing
And Play 14 Barry
Gibb Songs**

Spicks And Specks

**Turn Around …
Look At Us**

THE FESTIVAL ALBUMS COLLECTION 1965-1967
(2013 Festival)

The Bee Gees Sing And Play 14 Barry Gibb Songs
Track listing as 1965 album

Spicks And Specks
Track listing as 1966 album

Turn Around … Look At Us
Track listing as 1967 album

MORNING OF MY LIFE: THE BEST OF 1965-66
(2013 Festival)

Spicks And Specks
I Am The World
I Want Home
I Was A Lover, A Leader Of Men
How Love Was True
Morning Of My Life
Exit Stage Right
Jingle Jangle
Like Nobody Else
Butterfly
All By Myself
Glass House
Where Are You
Play Down
Second Hand People
And The Children Laughing
Wine And Women
I Don't Know Why I Bother With Myself
All Of My Life
How Many Birds
Coalman
Top Hat
The Storm
I'll Know What To Do

ROBIN GIBB
50 ST.CATHERINE'S DRIVE
(2014 Rhino)

Days of Wine and Roses
Instant Love
Alan Freeman Days
Wherever You Go
I Am the World
Mother of Love
Anniversary
Sorry
Cherish
Don't Cry Alone
Avalanche
One Way Love
Broken Wings
Sanctuary
Solid
All We Have Is Now
Sydney

Japanese edition bonus track
All That I Cherish (Demo)

E.S.P.

One

High Civilization

THE WARNER BROS. YEARS 1987 - 1991
(2014 Warner Bros)

E.S.P.
Track listing as 1987 album
Bonus Tracks
E.S.P. (Demo Version)
Angela (Edit)
E.S.P. (Edit)
You Win Again (Extended Version)
E.S.P. (Extended Version)

One
Track listing as 1989 album
Bonus Tracks
Shape Of Things To Come
One (Remix/Edit)
One (12" Dance Version)
One (12" Club Mix)

High Civilization
Track listing as 1991 album

One For All Concert 1989 Disc 1
Intro
Ordinary Lives
Giving Up The Ghost
To Love Somebody
I've Gotta Get A Message To You
One
Tokyo Nights
Words
Juliet
Lonely Days
New York Mining Disaster 1941
Holiday
Too Much Heaven
Heartbreaker
Islands In The Stream
Run To Me
World
Spicks And Specks
One For All Concert 1989 Disc 2
How Deep Is Your Love
It's My Neighborhood
How Can You Mend A Broken Heart
House Of Shame
I Started A Joke
Massachusetts
Stayin' Alive
Nights On Broadway
Jive Talkin'
You Win Again
You Should Be Dancing

1974-1979
(2015 Reprise)

Mr. Natural
Track listing as 1974 album

Main Course
Track listing as 1975 album

Children Of The World
Track listing as 1976 album

Spirits Having Flown
Track listing as 1979 album

The Miami Years
Stayin' Alive
How Deep Is Your Love
Night Fever
More Than A Woman
Emotion
Warm Ride
(Our Love) Don't Throw It All Away
If I Can't Have You
Rest Your Love On Me
It Doesn't Matter Much To Me
Stayin' Alive (Promo 12" Version)

ROBIN GIBB
SAVED BY THE BELL
(2015 Reprise)

Disc 1 - Robin's Reign ... Plus
August October
Gone Gone Gone
The Worst Girl In This Town
Give Me A Smile
Down Came The Sun
Mother And Jack
Saved By The Bell
Weekend
Farmer Ferdinand Hudson
Lord Bless All
Most Of My Life

Bonus Material
One Million Years
Hudson's Fallen Wind
Saved By The Bell (Mono)
Mother And Jack (Mono)
One Million Years (Mono)
Weekend (Mono)
August October (Mono)
Give Me A Smile (Mono)
Lord Bless All (Alternate Take)

Disc 2 - Sing Slowly Sisters - Sessions
Sing Slowly Sisters
Life
C'est La Vie, Au Revoir
Everything Is How You See Me
I've Been Hurt
Sky West And Crooked
Irons In The Fire
Cold Be My Days
Avalanche
Engines Aeroplanes
The Flag I Flew
Return To Austria
It's Only Make Believe
All's Well That Ends Well
A Very Special Day
Great Caesar's Ghost
Anywhere I Hang My Hat
Loud And Clear
Return To Austria (Demo)
Why Not Cry Together (Demo)

Disc 3 - Robin's Rarities
Alexandria Good Time
Janice
Love Just Goes
Agosto Ottobre (August October – sung in Italian)
Un Milione De Ani (One Million Years – sung in Italian)
Saved By The Bell (BBC Session)
Robin Talks To Brian Matthew (BBC)
August October (BBC Session)
Weekend (BBC Session)
Give Me A Smile (BBC Session)
Robin Talks With David Wigg (BBC)
The Band Will Meet Mr. Justice (Demo)
The People's Public Poke Song (Demo)
Indian Gin And Whiskey Dry (Demo)
The Girl To Share Each Day (Demo)
Heaven In My Hands (Demo)
Most Of My Life (Demo)
Goodbye Good World (Demo)
Down Came The Sun (Demo)
Don't Go Away (Demo)
Moon Anthem
Ghost Of Christmas Past

YOU SHOULD BE DANCING
(2015 Reprise)

Jive Talkin'
You Should Be Dancing
Love So Right
Stayin' Alive
Nights On Broadway
How Deep Is Your Love
Tragedy
(Our Love) Don't Throw It All Away
Night Fever
More Than A Woman
Fanny (Be Tender With My Love)
Spirits Having Flown
If I Can't Have You
Boogie Child
Love You Inside Out
Too Much Heaven
Emotion
Wind Of Change

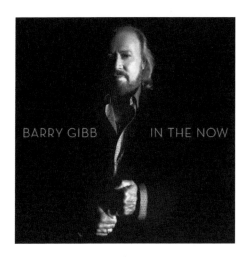

BARRY GIBB
IN THE NOW
(2016 Columbia)

In the Now
Grand Illusion
Star Crossed Lovers
Blowin' a Fuse
Home Truth Song
Meaning of the Word
Cross to Bear
Shadows
Amy in Colour
The Long Goodbye
Diamonds
End of the Rainbow

CD deluxe edition (bonus tracks)
Grey Ghost
Daddy's Little Girl
Soldier's Son

TIMELESS: THE ALL-TIME GREATEST HITS
(2017 Capitol)

Spicks and Specks
New York Mining Disaster 1941
To Love Somebody
Massachusetts
Words
I've Gotta Get a Message to You
I Started a Joke
Lonely Days
How Can You Mend a Broken Heart
Jive Talkin'
Nights on Broadway
Fanny (Be Tender with My Love)
You Should Be Dancing
How Deep Is Your Love
Stayin' Alive
Night Fever
More Than a Woman
Too Much Heaven
Tragedy
Love You Inside Out
You Win Again

BARRY GIBB

GREENFIELDS

(2021 Capitol)

I've Gotta Get a Message to You   (with Keith Urban)
Words of a Fool(with Jason Isbell)
Run to Me (with Brandi Carlile)
Too Much Heaven(with Alison Krauss)
Lonely Days (with Little Big Town)
Words (with Dolly Parton)
Jive Talkin' (with Miranda Lambert and Jay Buchanan)
How Deep Is Your Love (with Little Big Town and Tommy Emmanuel)
How Can You Mend a Broken Heart (with Sheryl Crow)
To Love Somebody (with Jay Buchanan)
Rest Your Love on Me (with Olivia Newton-John)
Butterfly (with David Rawlings and Gillian Welch)

Bonus tracks
With the Sun in My Eyes
Morning of My Life

MISCELLANEOUS & GUEST APPEARANCES

Bee Gees:
Gena's Theme

Barry Gibb: King Kathy/I Can Bring
Love/Summer Ends

Maurice Gibb: Laughing Child/Soldier
Johnny/Something's Blowing/Journey To
The Misty Mountains

Robin Gibb& Marcy Levy:
Help Me

Barry Gibb& Barbra Streisand:
Guilty/What Kind Of Fool

Barry Gibb& Barbra Streisand:
Guilty/What Kind Of Fool (Live)

Bee Gees:
Will You Love Me Tomorrow

Celine Dion & The Bee Gees:
Immortality

Bee Gees:
Ellan Vannin

Alistair Grinn& Robin Gibb:
My Lover's Prayer

Barry Gibb:
Love Is Blind

Barry Gibb& Barbra Streisand:
Come Tomorrow/Above The Law

G4 & Robin Gibb:
First Of May

US5 &Riobin Gibb:
Too Much Heaven

Valeria & Robin Gibb
Stayin' Alive

Barry Gibb:
Drown On The River

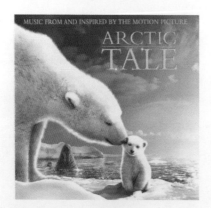

Barry Gibb:
Underworld

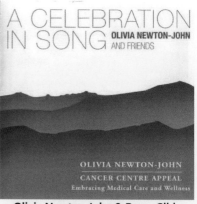

Olivia Newton John & Barry Gibb
The Heart Knows

Robin Gibb
Juliet (Live)

Rob Brydon, Ruth Jones, Sir Tom
Jomes& Robin Gibb:
Islands In The Stream

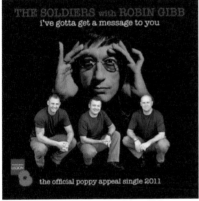

The Soldiers & Robin Gibb
I've Gotta Get A Message To You

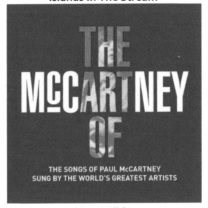

Barry Gibb:
When I'm Sixty Four

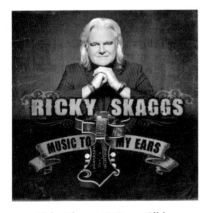

Ricky Skaggs & Barry Gibb:
Soldier's Son

Barry Gibb& Barbra Streisand:
If Only You Were Mine

SINGLES

Australian only singles (1963 – 1967)

The Battle Of The Blue And The Grey/The Three Kisses Of Love *(1963)*

Timber!/Take Hold Of That Star *(1963)*

Peace Of Mind/Don't Say Goodbye *(1964)*

Claustrophobia/Could It Be *(1964)*

Turn Around, Look At Me/Theme From the Travels Of Jamie McPheeters *(1964)*

House Without Windows/And I'll Be Happy (with Trevor Gordon) *(1965)*

Every Day I Have To Cry/You Wouldn't Know *(1965)*

Wine And Women/Follow The Wind *(1965)*

I Was A Lover, A Leader Of Men/And The Children Laughing *(1965)*

I Want Home/Cherry Red *(1966)*

Monday's Rain/All Of My Life *(1966)*

Spicks And Specks/I Am The World *(1966)*

Born A Man/Big Chance *(1967)*

UK singles

Spicks And Specks/I Am The World *(1967)*

New York Mining Disaster 1941/I Can't See Nobody *(1967)*

To Love Somebody/Close Another Door *(1967)*

Massachusetts/Barker Of The U.F.O. *(1967)*

World/Sir Geoffrey Saved The World *(1967)*

Words/Sinking Ships *(1968)*

Jumbo/The Singer Sang His Song *(1968)*

I've Gotta Get A Message To You/Kitty Can *(1968)*

First Of May/Lamplight *(1969)*

Tomorrow Tomorrow/Sun In My Morning *(1969)*

RG: Saved By The Bell/Mother And Jack *(1969)*

Don't Forget To Remember/The Lord *(1969)*

RG: One Million Years/Weekend *(1969)*

RG: August October/Give Me A Smile *(1970)*

I.O.I.O./Sweetheart *(1970)*

MG: Railroad/I've Come Back *(1970)*

BG: I'll Kiss Your Memory/This Time *(1970)*

Lonely Days/ Man For All Seasons *(1970)*

How Can You Mend A Broken Heart/Country Woman* *(1971)*

My World*/On Time* *(1972)*
Run To Me/Road To Alaska *(1972)*
Alive/Paper Mache Cabbages And Kings *(1972)*
Saw A New Morning/My Life Has Been A Song *(1973)*
Wouldn't I Be Someone/Elisa*(1973)*
Mr. Natural/It Doesn't Matter Much To Me*(1974)*
Charade/Heavy Breathing *(1974)*
Jive Talkin'/Wind Of Change *(1975)*
Nights On Broadway/Edge Of The Universe *(1975)*
Fanny (Be Tender With My Love)/Country Lane *(1976)*
You Should Be Dancing/Subway *(1976)*
Love So Right/You Stepped Into My Life *(1976)*
Children Of The World/Boogie Child *(1977)*
Edge Of The Universe *(Live)*/Words *(Live)* *(1977)*
How Deep Is Your Love/Can't Keep A Good Man Down (Live)*(1977)*
Stayin' Alive/If I Can't Have You*(1978)*
Night Fever/Down The Road *(Live)* *(1978)*
Too Much Heaven/Rest Your Love On Me *(1978)*
Tragedy/Until *(1979)*
Love You Inside Out/I'm Satisfied *(1979)*
Spirits (Having Flown)/Wind Of Change *(1980)*
RG: Help Me/Help Me *(Instrumental)* (with Marcy Levy) *(1980)*
BG: Guilty (with Barbra Streisand) *(1980)*
BG: What Kind Of Fool (with Barbra Streisand) *(1981)*
He's A Liar/ He's A Liar *(Instrumental)(1981)*
Living Eyes/I Still Love You *(1981)*
RG: Juliet/Hearts On Fire *(1983)*
The Woman In You/Stayin'Alive*(1983)*
Someone Belonging To Someone/I Love You Too Much
(Instrumental)(1983)
RG: Another Lonely Night In New York/I Believe In Miracles *(1983)*
RG: How Old Are You?/I Believe In Miracles *(1983)*
RG: Boys Do Fall In Love/Diamonds*(1984)*
RG: Secret Agent/Robot*(1984)*
BG: Shine Shine/She Says *(1984)*
MG: Hold Her In Your Hand/Hold Her In Your Hand (Instrumental)
(1984)
RG: Like A Fool/Possession*(1985)*
RG: Toys/Do You Love Her? *(1986)*
You Win Again/Backtafunk*(1987)*
E.S.P./Overnight *(1987)*
Crazy For Your Love/You Win Again *(Remix)* *(1988)*
Childhood Days/Moonlight Madness *(1988)*

Ordinary Lives/Wing And A Prayer *(1989)*
One/Flesh And Blood *(1989)*
Secret Love/True Confessions*(1991)*
When He's Gone/Massachusetts (*Live*) *(1991)*
The Only Love/You Win Again *(Live) (1991)*
Paying The Price Of Love/My Destiny *(1993)*
For Whom The Bell Tolls/Decadance*(1993)*
How To Fall In Love, Part 1/855 7019/Fallen Angel (*Remix*)*(1994)*
Alone/Rings Around The Moon *(1997)*
I Could Not Love You More/Love Never Dies/Brits Medley (*Live*)*(1997)*
Still Waters Run Deep/Still Waters Run Deep (*Demo*)/Obsessions*(1997)*
Ellan Vannin *(1998)*
Immortality (with Celine Dion)*(1998)*
This Is Where I Came In/Just In Case/I Will Be There *(2001)*
RG: Please/Watching You/Don't Rush *(2002)*
RG: Wait Forever/Wait Forever (Shanghai Surprise Remix)*(2003)*
RG: Lover's Prayer (with Alistair Griffin) *(2003)*
RG: First Of May (with G4) *(2005)*
BG: Doctor Mann (iTunes Download) *(2006)*
BG: Underworld (iTunes Download) *(2006)*
RG: Mother Of Love (musicload.de Download) *(2006)*
BG: Drown On The River (iTunes Download) *(2007)*
RG: Wing And A Prayer/To Love Somebody (robingibb.com Download) *(2008)*
RG: Ellan Vannin (Homecoming Mix) *(2008)*
RG: Islands In The Stream (with Rob Brydon, Ruth Jones & Tom Jones for Comic Relief) *(2009)*
All In Your Name (with Michael Jackson) (barrygibb.com Download) *(2011)*
RG: Sydney (robingibb.com Download) *(2011)*
RG: I've Gotta Get A Message To You (with The Soldiers) *(2011)*
BG: Grey Ghost (barrygibb.com Download) *(2011)*
BG: Daddy's Little Girl (barrygibb.com Download) *(2011)*

VIDEOS

CIC Video (1984)

Polygram Video (1984)

Hendring (1986)

Virgin Music Video (1985)

MGM/UA Home Video (1985)

Vision Video Limited (1985)

MPI Home Entertainment (1990)

MPI Home Entertainment (1990)

MPI Home Entertainment (1990)

Fan Association (1991)

Polygram Video (1997)

Image Entertainment (2001)

DVDs

Polygram Video (1997)
UK

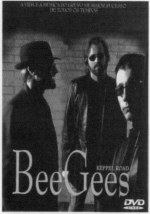

Cine Art (1998)
Brazil

MPI Hone Video (1997)
USA

Gema Discos e Fitas (1997)
Brazil

Eagle Vision (2018)
Europe

IMC Vision (2011)
UK

A&E Home Video (2001)
USA

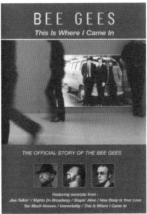

Eagle Vision (2001)
Europe

Eagle Vision (2001)
Europe

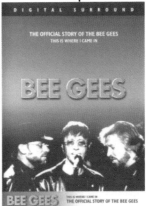

Vid.co.kr (2003)
South Korea

Dreamix (2003)
South Korea

Eagle Vision (2005)
Europe

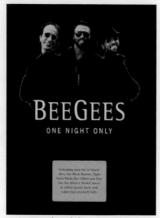

Eagle Vision (1998)
Europe

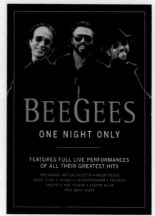

Eagle Vision (2013)
USA

Image Entertainment (2001)
UK

Standing Room Only (2007)
USA

Universal (2003)
USA

Eagle Vision (2010)
Europe

Duke Video (2011)
Isle of Man

Universal Pictures UK (2020)
UK

Universal (2005)
UK

BarryGibb.com (2006)
USA

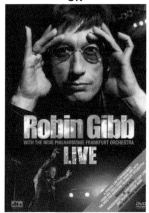

Eagle Vision (2005)
Europe

Eagle Vision (2011)
Europe

FURTHER READING

David Leaf
Octobus Books (1979)

David Leaf
Pinnacle Books (1980)

Kim Stevens
Quick Fox (1978)

Kim Stevens
Scholastic Book Services (1978)

Kim Stevens
Jove/HBJ (1979)

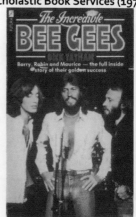

Dick Tatham
Futura Publications (1979)

Larry Pryce
Granada Publishing (1979)

Larry Pryce
Chelsea House (1980)

David English& Alex Brychta
EMMC (1979)

David English& Alex Brychta
Quartet Books (1983)

Andrew Sandoval
Retrofuture Day-By-Day (2012)

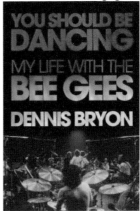

Dennis Bryon
ECW Books (2015)

Michael Henkels (German)
Taurus Press (1979)

Paul Sahner (German)
Bastai Lubbe (1979)

(German)
IVP Inland Presse (1979)

Petra Zeitz (German)
VIP Music (1992)

Norbert Lippe (German)
DrittlerDruck (1998)

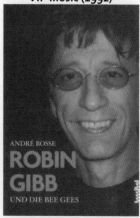

Andre Bosse (German)
Hannibal (2011)

Jordi Sierra i Fabra (Spanish)
Unilibro (1978)

Carlos Zanon (Spanish)
Ediciones Jucar (1998)

Jean-Jacques Jelot-Blanc (French)
Editions Gerard Cottreau (1978)

Silvia Guglielmi (Italian)
Lato Side (1981)

Eleuterio Langowski (Portugese)
Ciapress Editora (2008)

All editions: Melinda Bilyeu, Hector Cook, Andrew Môn Hughes
with assistance from Joseph Brennan & Mark Crohan

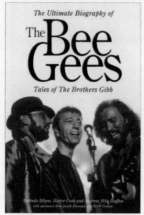

Omnibus Press – 1ˢᵗ Edition (2000)

Omnibus Press – 2ⁿᵈ Edition (2001)

Omnibus Press – 3ʳᵈ Edition (2003)

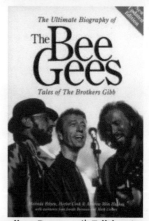

Omnibus Press – 4ᵗʰ Edition (2012)

Star St.Petersburg Press (Russian) (2005)

Star Cluster (German) (2007)

All editions by Andrew Môn Hughes, Grant Walters & Mark Crohan

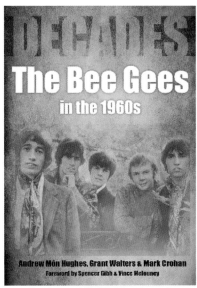

Sonicbond Publishing (2021)

Sonicbond Publishing (2022)

Coming 2022 from Sonicbond Publishing:
Decades: The Bee Gees in the 1980s
Decades: The Bee Gees in the 1990s

Printed in Great Britain
by Amazon